Special thanks to:

Deanna, Jon, Kristina, & Zayne
for their supporting art pieces.

Ms. Kate G, Ms. Kate P.
& Saint Margaret's
Third Grade Class for piloting
this book series.

Kids4Kids

Alexander	Eli	Kenneth	Natalie
Alyssa	Emerald	Koury	Sophia
Audrey	Evelyn	Lana	Sylvia
Clare	Finley	Madelyn	Vincent
Delayne	Gregory	Maura	Yoseline

Lord, have mercy. Christ have mercy. Lord, have mercy.
Christ hear us. Christ, graciously hear us.
God the Father of heaven, have mercy on us.
God the Son, Redeemer of the world, have mercy on us.
God the Holy Ghost, have mercy on us.
Holy Trinity, one God, have mercy on us.

After each Marian title,
say: Pray for us.

by Audrey F.
Age 4,
Wisconsin

Holy Mary
Holy Mother of God
Holy Virgin of Virgins
Mother of Christ
Mother of the Church
Mother of Mercy
Mother of Divine Grace
Mother of Hope
Mother Most Pure
Mother Most Chaste
Mother Inviolate
Mother Undefiled
Mother Most Amiable
Mother Most Admirable
Mother of Good Counsel

"Jesus is in
Mary's tummy."

"The snake
that Mary
crushes."

Mother of Our Creator
Mother of Our Savior
Virgin Most Prudent
Virgin Most Venerable
Virgin Most Renowned

Catholic Kids4Kids
Litany of Loreto Book Series

Mary, Mystical Rose
Pray for us!

Featuring:
Eve, Mother of Mankind
Saint Bridget of Sweden
Saint Thérèse of Lisieux
The Virtue of Patience

"It is an act of justice due to the eternal
God... that parents are naturally bound to
instruct their children from their
infancy in this knowledge of God and to
direct them with solicitous care, so
they at once may see their ultimate end
and seek it in their first acts
of intellect and will."
- Blessed Mary of Agreda

Front Cover Kids4Kids' Art:
Crucifix with Rose & Saint Thérèse quote
by Sophia V, Age 5, California

Back Cover Kids4Kids' Art:
Mary, Mystical Rose
by Evelyn P, Age 5, Wyoming

The publishers have presented everything as free
from Catholic doctrinal error as possible.

Text quotes were preserved as much as possible,
but in some cases adapted for space and a younger
audience with every intention of keeping the
integrity of the original meaning.

Additional Art Attribution and Bibliography
may be found at the end of the book.

Virgin Most Faithful
Mirror of Justice
Seat of Wisdom
Cause of Our Joy
Spiritual Vessel
Vessel of Honor
Singular Vessel of Devotion

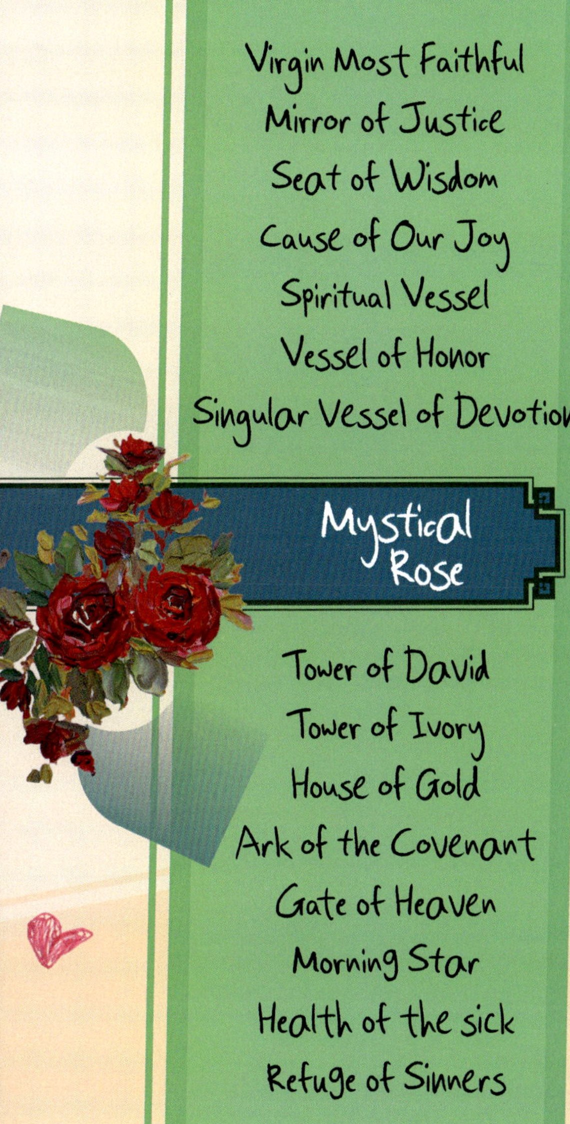

Mystical Rose

Tower of David
Tower of Ivory
House of Gold
Ark of the Covenant
Gate of Heaven
Morning Star
Health of the sick
Refuge of Sinners

Solace of Migrants
Comfort of the Afflicted
Help of Christians
Queen of Angels
Queen of Patriarchs
Queen of Prophets
Queen of Apostles
Queen of Martyrs
Queen of Confessors
Queen of Virgins
Queen of all Saints
Queen Conceived Without Original Sin
Queen Assumed into Heaven
Queen of the Most Holy Rosary
Queen of Families
Queen of Peace

Lamb of God, who takes away the sins of the world, spare us, O Lord. Lamb of God, who takes away the sins of the world, graciously hear us, O Lord. Lamb of God, who takes away the sins of the world, have mercy on us.

Pray for us, O Holy Mother of God. That we may be made worthy of the promises of Christ.

Let us pray. Grant, we beseech thee, O Lord God, that we, your servants, may enjoy perpetual health of mind and body; and by the glorious intercession of the Blessed Mary, ever Virgin, may be delivered from present sorrow, and obtain eternal joy. Through Christ our Lord. Amen.

How many of the Litany of Loreto titles do you know ?

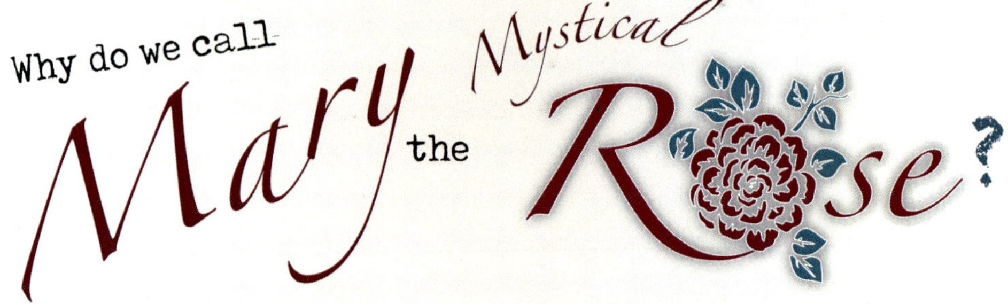

Let's start at the very beginning!

Genesis

And the Lord God formed **man** out of the **SLIME**

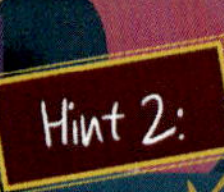

of the **earth:**

and breathed into his face the **breath of life**, and **man** became a **living soul.**

God
Soul
Soul

God created man.
Natalie F. Age 2, Wisconsin

Adam and Eve

Adam and Eve. - Vincent V. Age 3, California

Eve was made out of Adam's rib.

And God created man to His own image: to the image of God He created him.

Male and Female: He created them.

Creation of Adam - Michelangelo, 1511 A.D.

The Creation, 1490 A.D.

What else did God make?

A Stork, 1260 A.D.

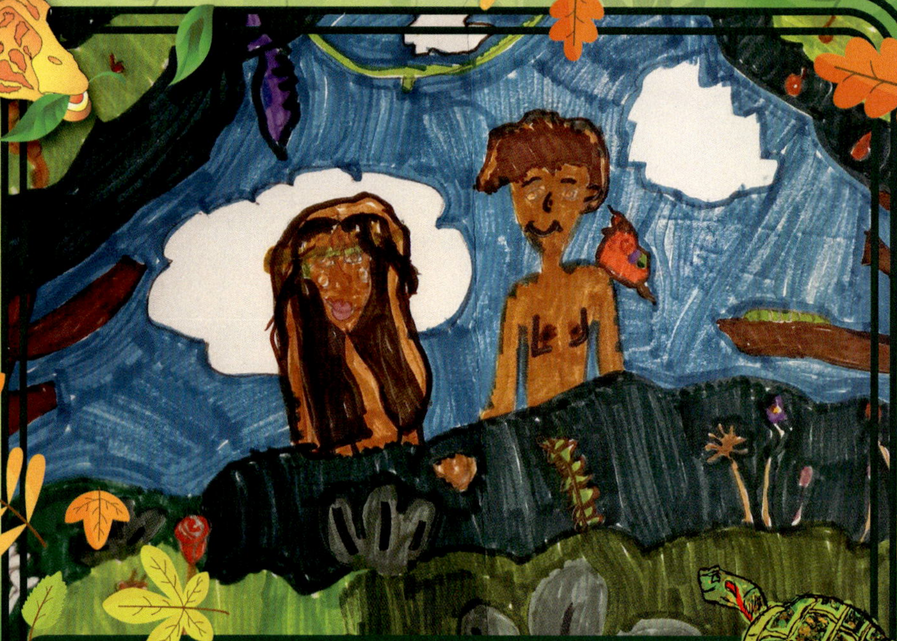

God created the world and Adam and Eve
Emerald M., & Yoseline P., Ages 8, Wyoming

The Lord God had planted the Garden of Eden, where He placed man whom He had formed. And the Lord God brought forth from the ground all kinds of trees, beautiful to behold, and pleasant to eat.

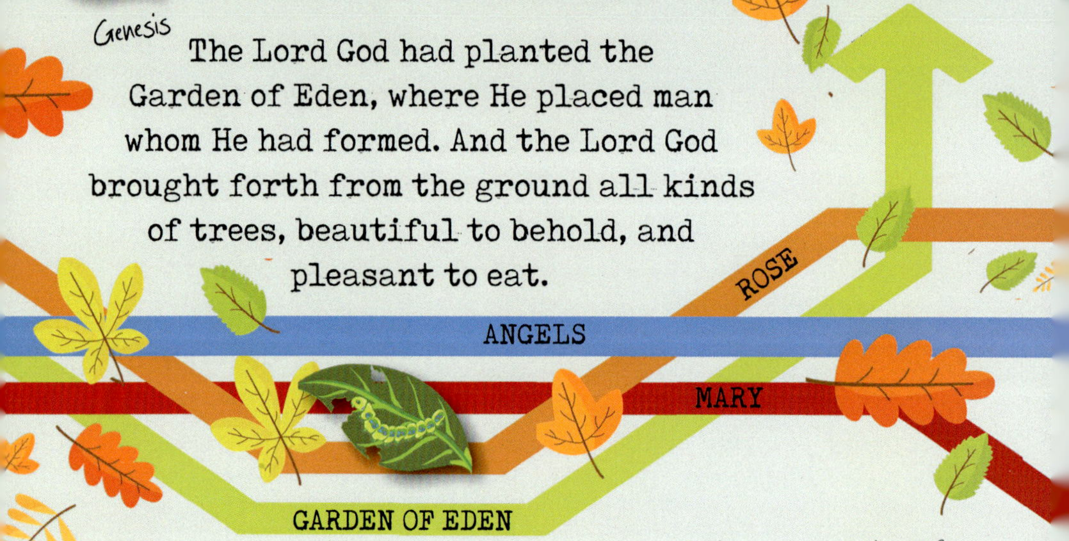

How many of each leaf?

□ = ☐ □ = ☐ □ = ☐ □ = ☐ □ = ☐

God created the world and created Adam and Eve. He gave them the world to use! He gave them the world to live in! He gave them water. The devil tempted Eve to eat the fruit of the garden and disobey God. She shared the fruit with Adam. Because they sinned...

Creation of the Garden of Eden
Madelyn F. Age 3, Wisconsin

Can you draw shape animals?

The caption below the illustration:

Creation of the Angels, Fidelis Schabet, 1874 A.D.

The Story of the Angels

By Blessed Mary of Ágreda
Adapted from the City of God

CREATION and the FALL of LUCIFER

God created heaven for angels & men;
the earth as a place of pilgrimage for men.

Although the angels were created in the heavens, they still needed to pass a test.

1) They were commanded to adore God as their Creator.

The good angels offered God their love, & will freely with joy.

Lucifer loved himself. He obeyed grudgingly.

The angels learned that God was to create mankind - creatures lower than themselves. Man was to be in high favor, so much so, that the 2nd Person of the Blessed Trinity was to assume man's nature. God instructed the angels on the justice of this.

All the holy angels submitted themselves in humility and love.

But Lucifer, full of envy and pride, resisted.

They were commanded to adore as their superior, a <u>woman</u>, in whose womb the God-man was to be born. This woman would become the

<u>Queen of Heaven.</u>

The good angels by agreeing to adore her became more humble, and praised the power of the Most High.

Lucifer, however, rose to an <u>even higher</u> level of pride. Enraged, he aspired to be the head of angels and mankind. If there was to be a creature-union with God, he wanted it to be with him! He vowed that he would set up a kingdom independent from the 2nd Person of the Trinity.

Lucifer's rebellion angered the Lord. God said:

*This woman will crush your head!
You will be destroyed by her!*

If, through your pride, **death** enters the world,
then, life will enter through the humility of this woman.
*Mankind will enjoy the gifts which you and your followers
have lost.*

Then happened that great battle in heaven.

*Saint Michael and the holy angels fought
against Lucifer and his followers. This is
described by the apostle, Saint John,
in the Scriptures.*

Apocalypse

Behold there appeared a great red
dragon having 7 heads and crowns, and
10 horns.

And his tail brought down a third of the stars of heaven.

The dragon stood before the woman, who was about to give birth; that, he might devour her Son, who was to rule all.

3) The good angels, persevering in grace, merited eternal happiness.

When He was born, the Son was taken up to God, and to His throne. The woman fled into the wilderness where she had a place prepared by God.

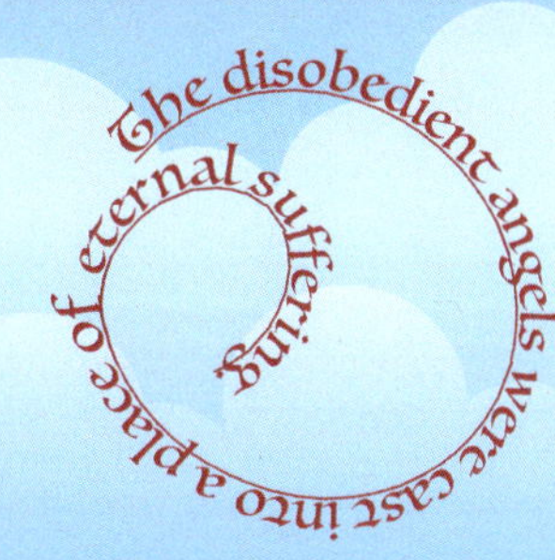

WHO IS LIKE GOD?
"I saw Lucifer like lightning fall from heaven!"
-Jesus
Saint Michael Vanquishing Lucifer by Raphael 1518 A.D.

Which one is the Woman in the vision?

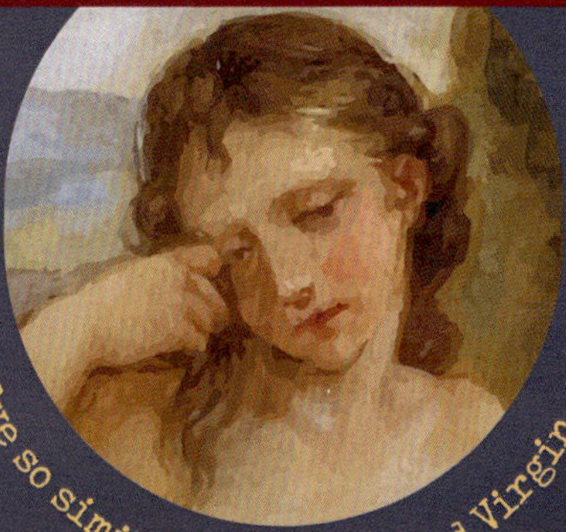

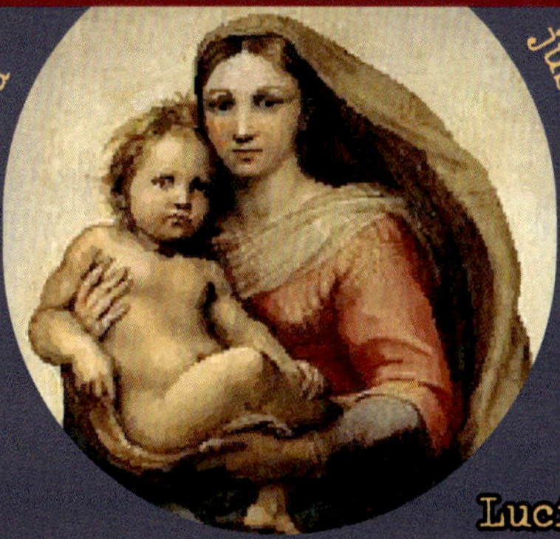

God formed Eve so similar to the Blessed Virgin, that she looked just like Her.

Blessed Mary of Ágreda

Lucifer had mixed them up! The Lord hid from him the fact that Eve was made from Adam's rib.

Lucifer envied mankind. He impatiently waited for their creation. He plotted to ruin them.

When Lucifer saw them, he thought that Adam had been born from Eve. He thought that she was the Woman, and Adam was the God-man that he had seen in the heavens.

He took the form of a serpent, and drew Eve into a conversation, which she should not have had.

Eve began to believe his lies. Then she disobeyed the command of God. She persuaded her husband likewise to sin. Then ruin overtook them.

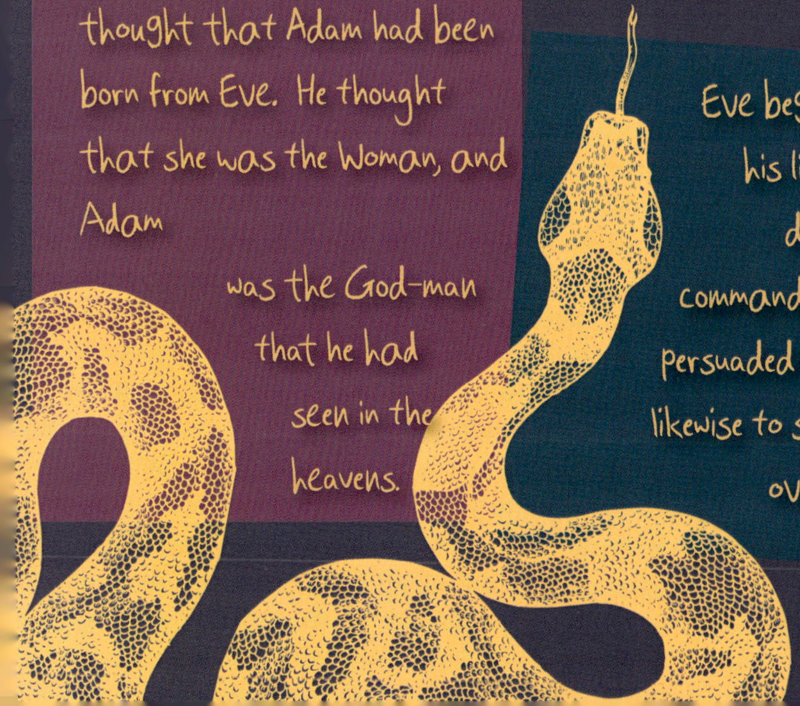

The Fall of Adam and Eve
Audrey F. Age 4, Wisconsin

Foot & Toe Print Tree
Gregory F. Age 6 mo, Georgia
Alexander F. Age 2, Georgia

God created the world and created Adam and Eve. He gave them the world to USE! He gave them the world to live in! He gave them water. The devil tempted Eve to eat the fruit of the garden and disobey God. She shared the fruit with Adam.

But God found them.
God asked: "Why have you disobeyed Me?"

Adam said: "Eve told me to."

Eve said: "The serpent lied to me."

God said to the serpent: "Because you have tricked them, you will crawl on your belly and the Woman will crush your head!"

Saint Ambrose says that the rose grew in the Garden without thorns. Only after man's fall, it grew the thorns to remind man of his disobedience.

The rose remained beautiful & fragrant to remind the w of Eden.

The rose

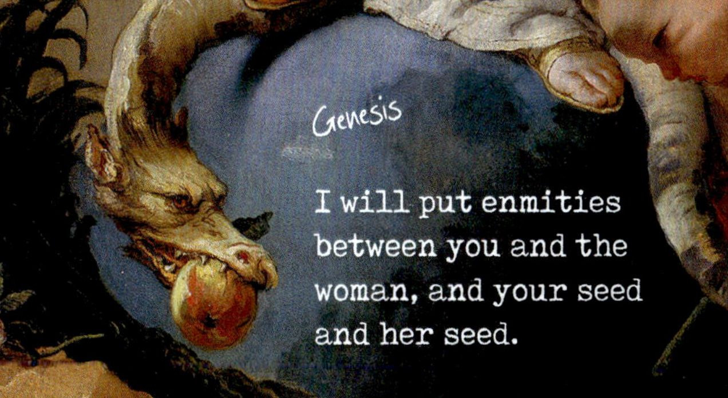

Genesis

I will put enmities between you and the woman, and your seed and her seed.

To Eve, He said: "In sorrow you will bring forth children, and you will be under your husband."

To Adam, He said: "Because you listened to your wife, and have eaten of the tree that I commanded you not to eat, cursed is the earth.

Now you have to work to eat. The earth will produce thorns for you. You will also die and return to dust."

And the Lord God made for Adam and his wife, garments of skins, and clothed them. And the Lord God sent them out of Eden.

God placed before the Garden, angels with a flaming sword, to protect the Tree of Life.

They lost the happy position, in which God had placed them. for themselves, and all of mankind.

Thank you for reading about the Garden of Eden.

When Lucifer saw their interior beauty changed into the ugliness of sin, he celebrated his triumph. But he soon fell from his proud boasting when he saw the merciful love of God.

God offered them a chance of doing penance by giving them hope of pardon. They disposed themselves toward this forgiveness by sorrow and contrition.

Eve was the first mother, and her children were named Cain and Abel and Seth.

Adam and Eve After the Fall!
Koury C, Age 9, Wyoming

Since the middle ages, the traditional feast of Saints Adam and Eve has been celebrated on Christmas Eve!

DID YOU KNOW?

In the Middle Ages, Catholics performed a "Paradise Play" to celebrate the feast of Saints Adam and Eve. They would hang apples on the tree to symbolize the fruit eaten in the Garden. The play ended with the promise of the birth of Jesus, which is celebrated the next morning on Christmas.

CAN YOU ANSWER THESE QUESTIONS?

What has happened to us on account of the sin of Adam?

On account of the sin of Adam, we, his descendants, come into the world deprived of sanctifying grace and inherit his punishment, as we would have inherited his gifts had he been obedient to God.

What is this sin in us called?

This sin in us is called original.

Baltimore Catechism

Why is this sin called original?

This sin is called original because it comes down to us through our origin, or descent, from Adam.

Did God abandon man after Adam fell into sin?

God did not abandon man after Adam fell into sin, but promised to send into the world a Saviour to free man from his sins and to reopen to him the gates of heaven.

Who is the Saviour of all men?

The Saviour of all men is Jesus Christ.

The Blessed Virgin Mary was preserved from original sin in view of the merits of her Divine Son, and this privilege is called her

Immaculate Conception.

Madonna Adoring the Child with Musical Angels
- Bernardino Zenale, 1510 A.D.

Mary was created from all time to be the Mother of God. The angels in heaven who saw her perfect soul being created were happy and praised God.

Mama Mary & Happy faces
Clare V, Age 2, California

Before I formed thee in the womb of thy mother, I knew thee: and before thou came out of the womb, I sanctified thee.
- Jeremiah

Why did Mary receive this special grace?

Mary received this special grace in order to be the Mother of God because she needed to be perfectly pure.

How was the Son of God made man?

The Son of God was conceived and made man by the power of the Holy Ghost in the womb of the Blessed Virgin Mary.

When was the Son of God conceived and made man?

The Son of God was conceived and made man on Annunciation Day, the day on which the Angel Gabriel announced to the Blessed Virgin Mary that she was to be the Mother of God.

For God so loved the world, as to give His only-begotten Son, that whosoever believeth in Him may not perish, but may have life everlasting.
— Saint John

She whose sinless soul was filled with the Divine Spirit of Jesus Christ, who in the name of the whole human race gave her consent for a spiritual marriage between the Son of God and human nature.

Pope Pius XII

For into Eve, as yet a virgin, had crept the word which was the framer of death, equally into a virgin was to be introduced the Word of God which was the builder-up of life.
— Tertullian

"Eve was a thorn, wounding, bringing death to all: in Mary we see a rose, soothing everybody's hurts, giving the destiny of salvation back to all."

- Saint Bernard of Clairvaux

December 8th is the feast of the Immaculate Conception!

Through Eve, the beautiful and desirable glory of men was extinguished, but it has revived through Mary."

- Saint Ephrem of Syrus

Mary is the New Eve.

Read about Mary's "yes"!

How are
these
the same?

How are
they
different?

Can you draw Mary?

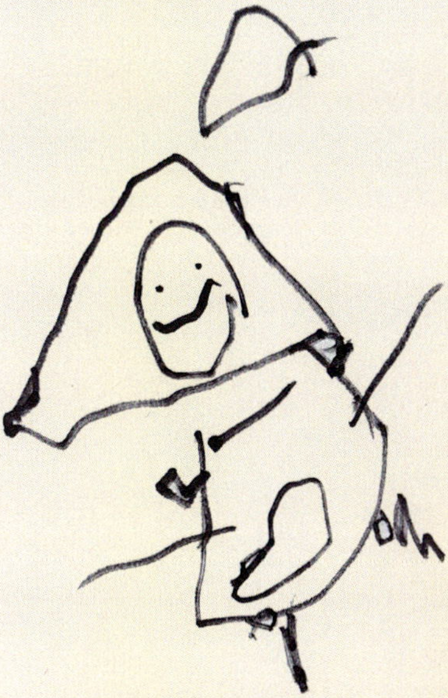

Mary with baby Jesus
in her tummy and a halo.
Madelyn F. Age 3, Wisconsin

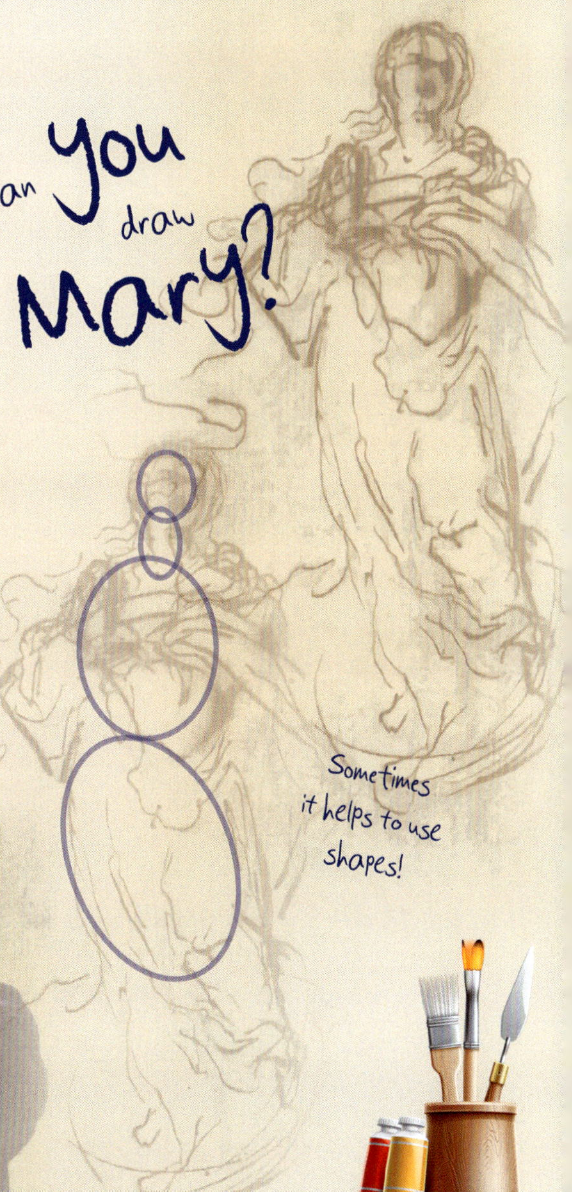

Sometimes
it helps to use
shapes!

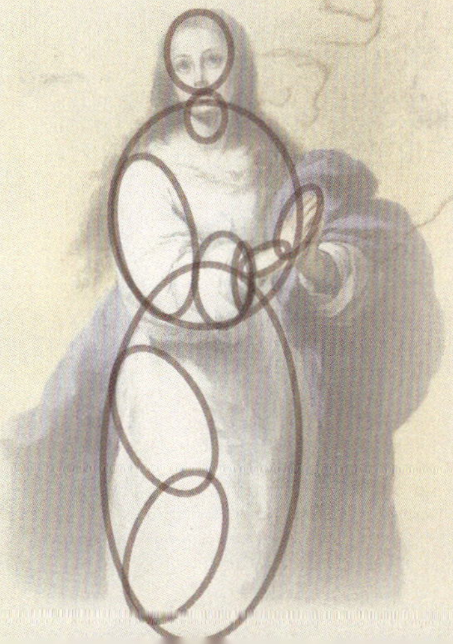

Mary said to Saint Bridget:

"I am she who heard the truth from the lips of Gabriel and believed without doubting. This is why Truth took for Himself flesh and blood from my body and remained in me."

Saint Bridget of Sweden
Sylvia P., Age 9, Wyoming

Keep reading to the end to learn more about Saint Bridget!

The Annunciation

Adapted from the Prophesies and Revelations of Saint Bridget. She had a vision of the Annunciation from Mary's perspective.

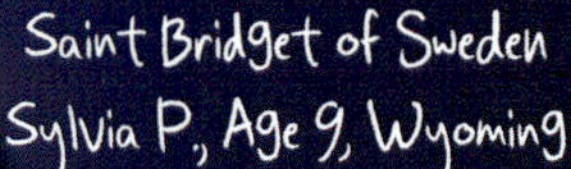

I am the Queen of Heaven.

Love my Son, for He is most worthy; when you have Him, you have all that is worthwhile. I want to tell you how wonderful His love for my body and soul was. My Son loved me before I loved Him, since He is my Creator. When my body had been made and formed, God infused my soul into it from His divinity, and my soul was immediately sanctified along with my body, and the angels guarded and served me day and night.

Nothing was pleasing to me but God! I always wished in my heart to live until the time of His birth, and perhaps, deserve to become the unworthy handmaid of the Mother of God.

I also promised in my heart to keep my virginity, if this was acceptable to Him, and to have no possessions in the world. However, if God wanted otherwise, my will was that His will, not mine, be done; for I believed that He could do all things and that He wanted nothing but what was best for me.

Therefore, I entrusted all my will to Him.

An inspiration about God's great power came over me, and I recalled how the angels and everything created serve Him, and how His glory is indescribable and unlimited.

An angel of God appeared before me, and he said to me:

"Hail, full of grace,
the Lord is with thee!"

When I heard this, I wondered what he meant and why he had come to me with such a greeting, for I knew and believed that I was unworthy of any such thing – or any good thing! However, I also knew that nothing is impossible for God, if He desires it.

Then the angel spoke again: "The child to be born in you is holy and will be called the Son of God."

Be it done unto me
according to thy
word.
- Saint Luke
The Annunciation
- Luca Giordano, 1672 A.D.

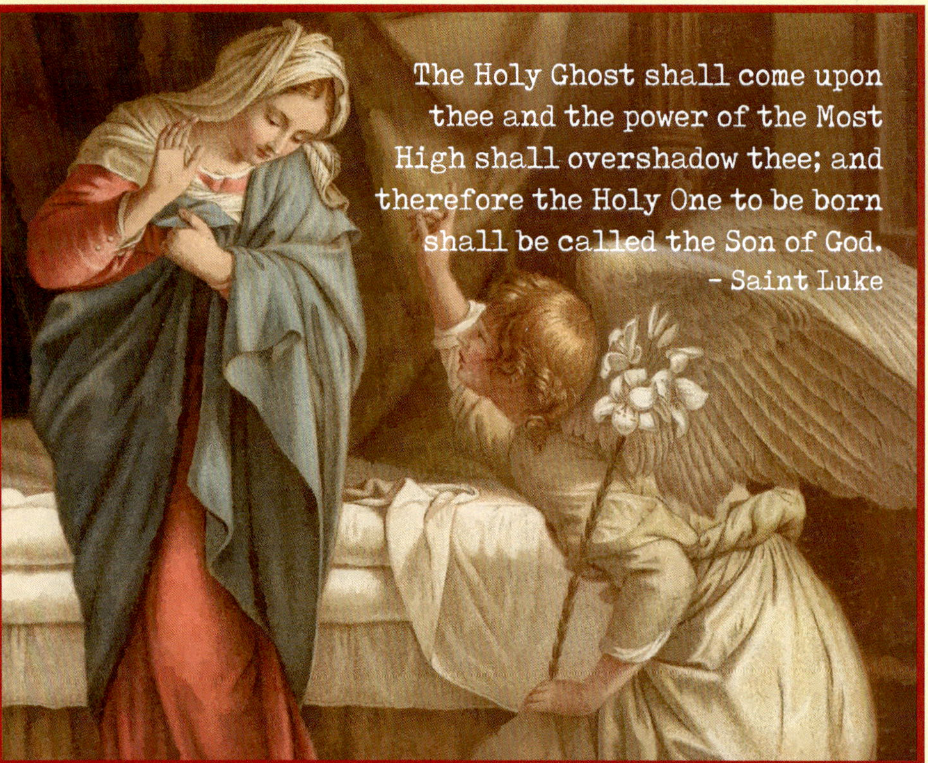
The Holy Ghost shall come upon thee and the power of the Most High shall overshadow thee; and therefore the Holy One to be born shall be called the Son of God.
- Saint Luke

But, not even then did I consider myself worthy, and I did not ask the angel why, or when, this would happen. Instead I asked him how it could be that I, an unworthy maiden, who did not know any man, should become the Mother of God.

The angel answered me: "Nothing is impossible for God, for whatever He wants to do will be done."

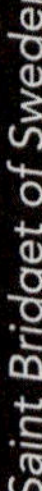

When I had heard these words of the angel, I felt the most fervent desire to become the Mother of God, and my soul spoke out of love and desire, saying: 'God's will be done in me!'

Saint Bridget of Sweden

With these words, my Son was conceived in my womb to the joy of my soul and my every limb!

I bore Him without any pain, without any heaviness or discomfort.

I humbled myself in all things, knowing that He whom I bore was the Almighty!

Saint Bridget of Sweden

When I gave birth to Him, it was also without any pain or sin, just as I had conceived Him, but with such joy of soul and body that my feet did not feel the ground where they had been standing!

Just as He had entered my limbs to the joy of all my soul, He left my body, leaving my virginity intact, and my soul and whole body in a state of indescribable joy and jubilation.

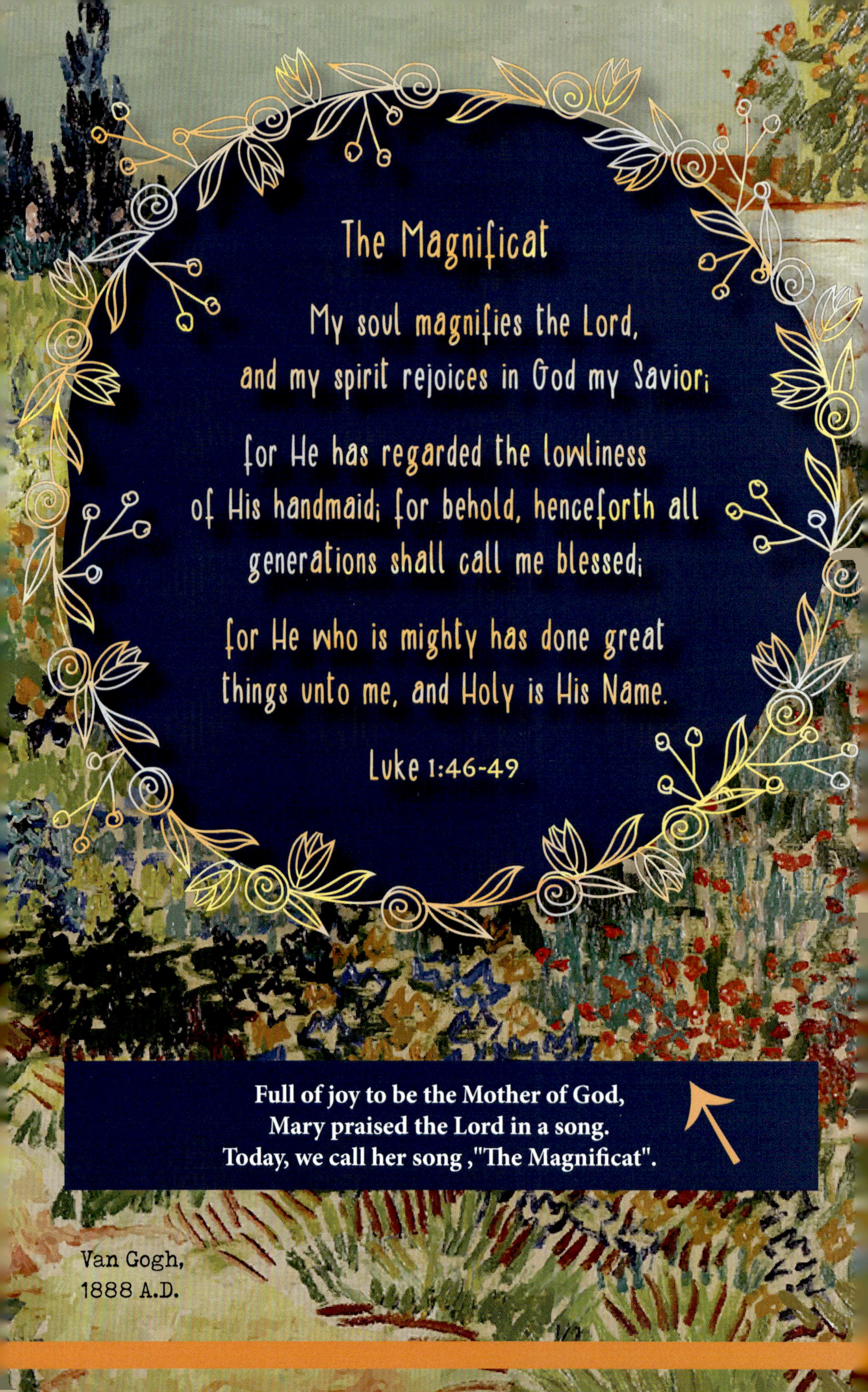

The Magnificat

My soul magnifies the Lord,
and my spirit rejoices in God my Savior;

for He has regarded the lowliness
of His handmaid; for behold, henceforth all
generations shall call me blessed;

for He who is mighty has done great
things unto me, and Holy is His Name.

Luke 1:46-49

Full of joy to be the Mother of God,
Mary praised the Lord in a song.
Today, we call her song ,"The Magnificat".

Van Gogh,
1888 A.D.

When I gazed upon and contemplated His beauty, joy seeped through my soul like dew drops and I knew myself to be unworthy of such a Son. But when I considered the places where (as I had learned from the predictions of the prophets) nails would be pierced through His hands and feet at the crucifixion, my eyes filled with tears and my heart was almost torn apart by sorrow.

Saint Bridget of Sweden

When my Son saw my weeping eyes, He became almost deathly saddened. However, when I considered His divine power, I was consoled again in knowing that this was what He wanted and that it should happen in this way, and I joined all my will to His. So my joy was always mixed with sorrow.

The Son answered: "Blessed be you, my most beloved Mother! My angel Gabriel said to you: 'Blessed art thou, Mary among women!' And I bear witness to you that you are blessed and most holy above all the choirs of angels.

You are like a flower in a garden that is surrounded by other fragrant flowers, but surpasses them all in scent, beauty, and virtue."

Van Gogh, 1889 A.D.

Did you know?

Scripture uses **GARDENS** as an example of **heaven** & its Saints.

Flowers & fruits are meant, in a mystical sense, as an example of the gifts & graces of the Holy Ghost.

A GARDEN is considered to be a place of spiritual peace, refreshment, & delight.

— Saint Cardinal Henry Newman

When we see a beautiful object,
a beautiful garden, or a beautiful flower,
let us think that there we behold a ray
of the infinite beauty of God, who has
given existence to that object.

- Saint Alphonsus Liguori

Lo, how a rose
e'er blooming!

- German Advent hymn

This is a reference to the Old Testament
prophecies of Isaiah, who predicts
the Incarnation of Jesus Christ.

It is also a reference to the Tree of Jesse,
a symbol of Jesus' lineage.

Van Gogh,
1888 A.D.

The Rose

gives a fragrant odor. It is beautiful to behold and tender to touch, and yet it grows among thorns.

The Rose is the most beautiful flower in all of Creation!

So may also those who are mild, **patient**, and beautiful in virtue, be put to a test among adversaries.

As the **thorn guards**, so do wicked surroundings protect the just against sin by demonstrating to them the destructiveness of sin."

- Mary to Saint Bridget

Mary Mystical Rose
Evelyn P. Age 5, Wyoming

Mary is the most beautiful flower ever seen in the spiritual world.

It is by God's grace that from this barren & desolate earth, there sprung up any flowers of holiness & glory.

She is the Mystical Rose.

Mystical means hidden.

And Mary is the Queen of them all.

She is the Queen of spiritual flowers and is called the Rose, for the rose is the most beautiful.

- Saint Cardinal Henry Newman

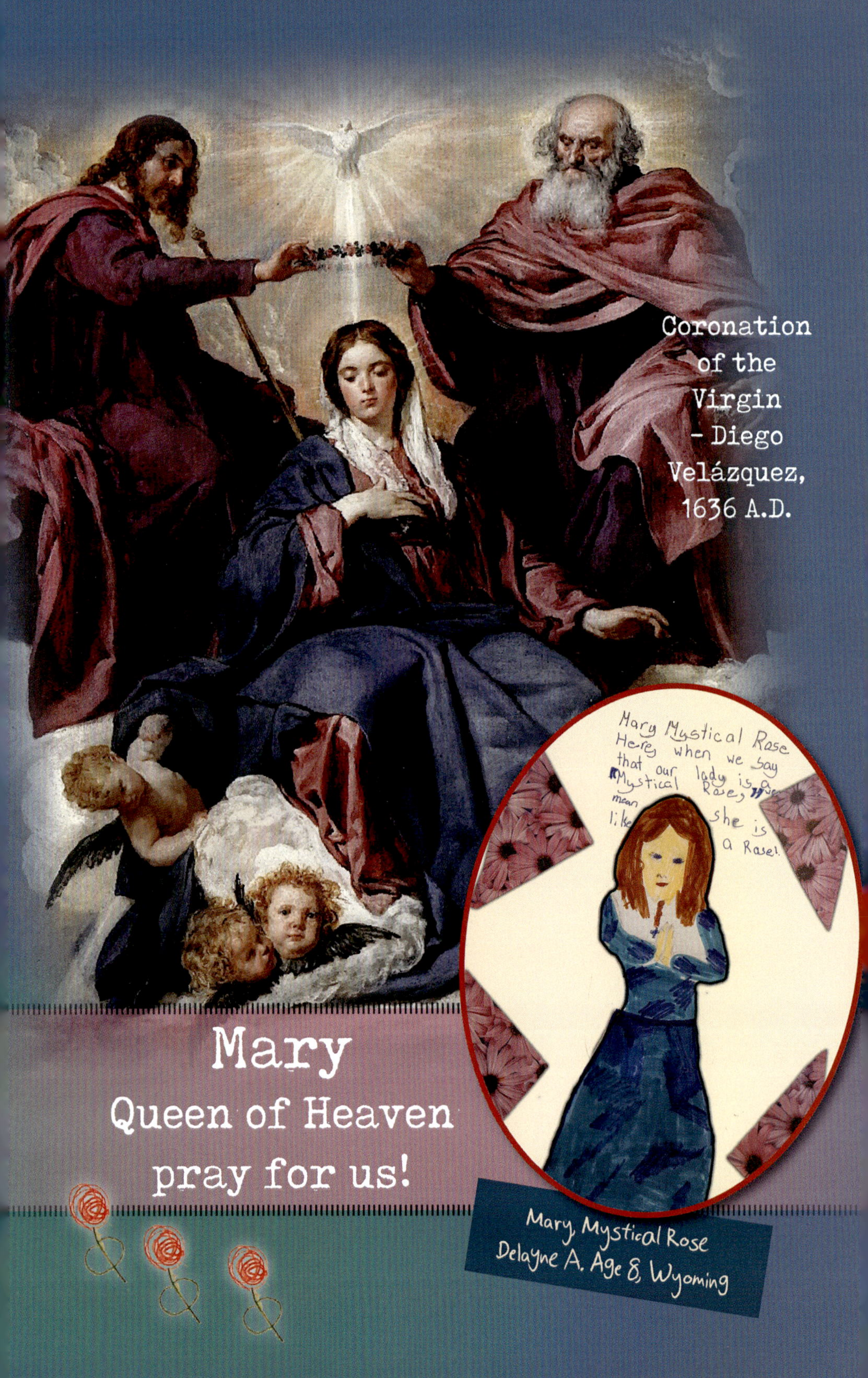

Mary
Queen of Heaven
pray for us!

Mary Mystical Rose
Delayne A. Age 8, Wyoming

Mystical means hidden.

Is it conceivable that they who had been so reverent and careful of the bodies of the saints and martyrs should neglect her – her who was the Queen of Martyrs and the Queen of the Saints, who was the Mother of the Lord? It is impossible.

Why then is she the hidden rose?

Plainly because that sacred body is in heaven, not on earth.

– Saint Cardinal Henry Newman

Jesus always listens to her!

Mary is the Mediatrix of All Graces. She distributes them
"whenever she wishes, to whom she wishes, how she wishes,
and how much she wishes." – Saint Bernard of Clairvaux

Jesus appeared to Saint Bridget and said:

Always prefer My Will before your own, because my Mother, your Lady, has, from the beginning to the end, never wanted anything but what I wanted. So love me alone, and you will have all the things you want, and you will have them in abundance.

Mary said to her Son, Jesus:

"Oh, my Lord and most dear Son, You were in my womb as true God and man. By your grace you sanctified me, who was but an earthen vessel. I beg you, have mercy on them once more!"

Then the Lord answered His Mother:

"Blessed be the words of your mouth that ascend like a sweet fragrance to God. You are the Queen and glory of angels and all saints because, by you, God and all the saints are made happy! Because your will was as my own from the beginning of your youth, I will do as you wish once more."

Each time you say a

Hail Mary

you are giving Mary a beautiful Rose!

Hail Mary, full of grace, the Lord is with thee. Blessed art thou amongst women and blessed is the fruit of thy womb, Jesus.

Holy Mary, Mother of God, pray for us sinners now and at the hour of our death. Amen.

Mary, Mystical Rose
Lana G. Age 8, Wyoming

Challenge!!!

Can you say 1 Hail Mary?

How about 5?

How about 10?

Did you know?

A Rosary, creates for Mary, a crown of roses!

When you say 1 Our Father, 10 Hail Marys, and 1 Glory Be, you are saying a DECADE of the Rosary.

Joan de Joanes – The Immaculate Conception

"I am the Rose of Sharon" - Song of Songs

And there shall come forth a rod out of the root of Jesse,
and a flower shall rise up out of his root. - Isaiah

You can also give

Mary beautiful flowers

by doing good deeds!

Mary, Mystical Rose
Finley T, Age 8, Wyoming

Saint Thérèse, as a young girl, wanted to make sacrifices. She made a chaplet so that she could keep track of her good deeds.

Learn more about her and how to make "good deed beads" on the next few pages.

For as often as we greet Mary with the angelic salutation, 'full of grace,' we present to the Blessed Virgin, in the repetition of our words of praise, roses which emit the most delightful perfume. – Pope Leo XIII

A Garden in September
Mary Hiester Reid,
1889 A.D.

Miss no opportunity of making some small sacrifice!
A smile. A kindly word. All for love. All for Jesus.

Saint Zélie, Saint Thérèse's mother, said:
Even Thérèse wants to start making sacrifices now. Marie has given each of the little ones a chaplet on which they can keep count of their good deeds. The most charming thing of all is to see Thérèse slip her hand into her pocket time and time again and move a bead along as she makes some sacrifice.

Our mortifications...
are like so many beautiful
flowers, that send up a perfume
extremely sweet before the Divine
Majesty.

– Saint Frances De Sales

1. Pull a string through a Crucifix or medal.

2. Make a knot.

3. Pull the string through one side of a bead.

4. Pull the other end of the string through the opposite side of the same bead.

5. Alternate the sides of the beads that the strings go through until you string up 10 beads.

6. Leave enough room for the beads to move up and down. Tie a 2nd knot.

7. Optional: Add a safety pin, clasp or another medal through or after the knot.

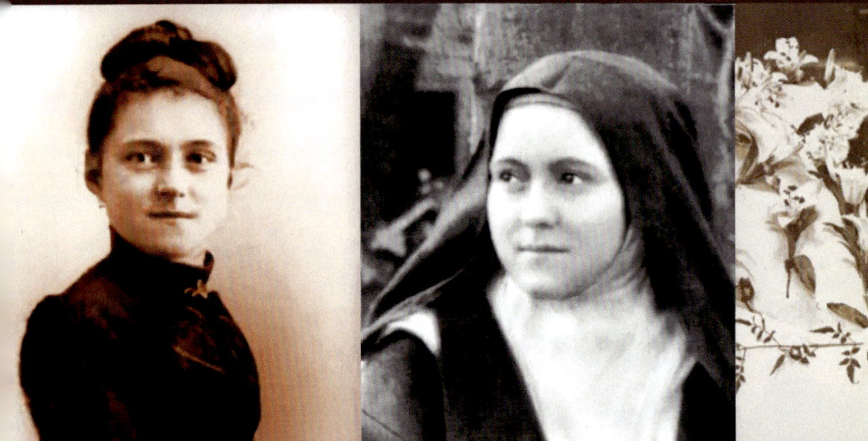

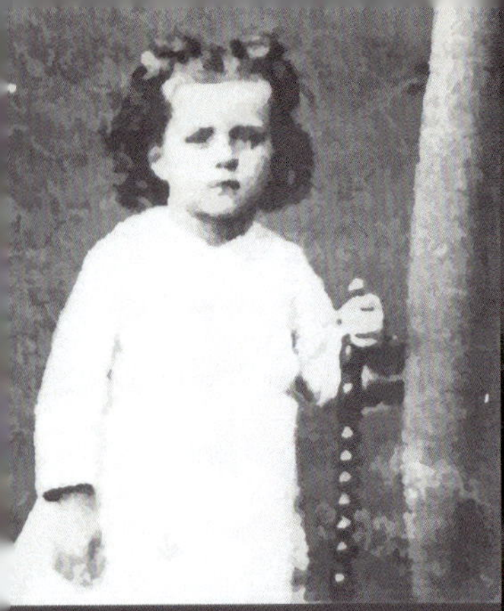
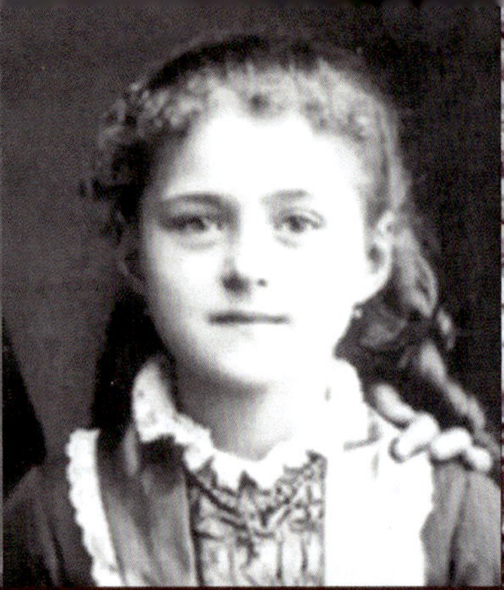
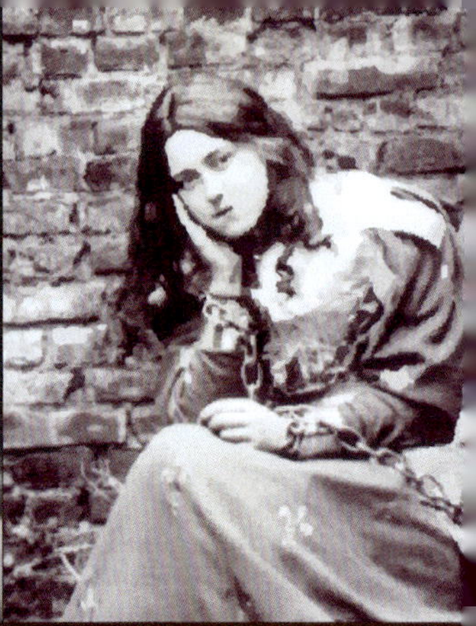
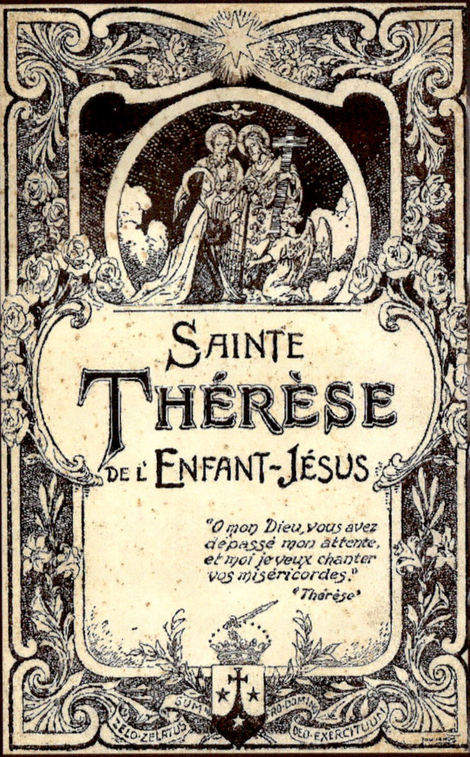
SAINTE
THÉRÈSE
DE L'ENFANT-JÉSUS
"O mon Dieu, vous avez dépassé mon attente, et moi je veux chanter vos miséricordes."
"Thérèse"
ZELO·ZELATUS
SUM
DEO·EXERCITUUM
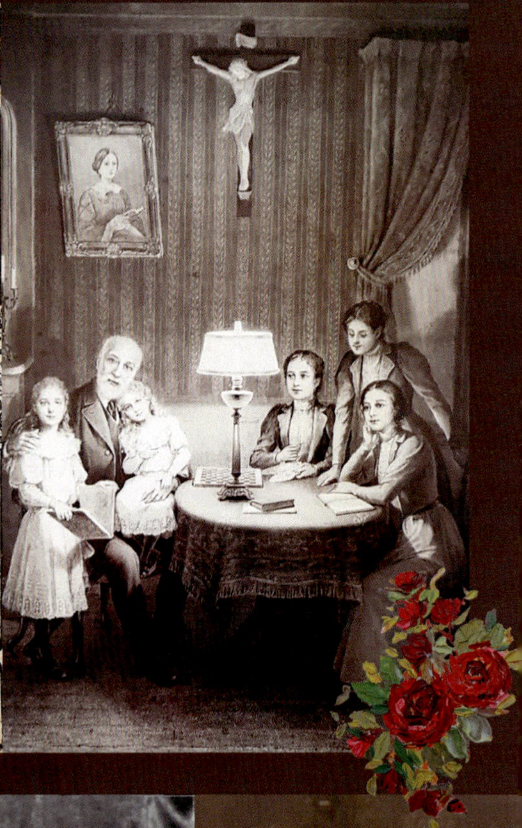
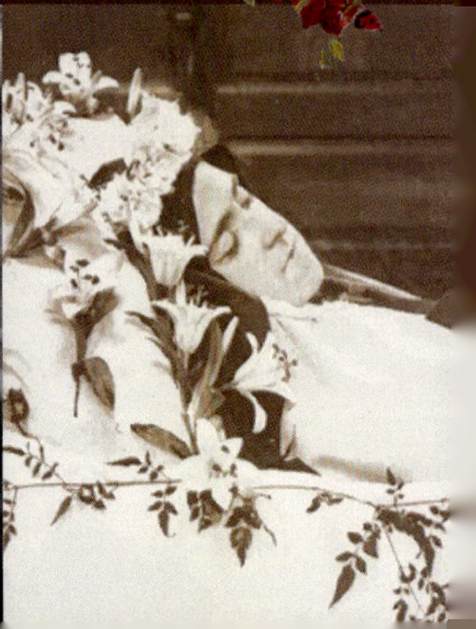

Au
soir de
cette
vie
je serai
jugée
sur
l'Amour

Rose on Crucifix
Sophia V., Age 5, California

Saint Thérèse's poems and prayers helped to spread the devotion to the Holy Face of Jesus.

"Make me resemble you, Jesus!"

MY PEACE & MY JOY
My joy I find in pain and loss,
I love the thorns
that guard
the rose; with joy
I kiss each heavy
cross, and smile with every
tear that flows.

start

Can you get to the center of the rose?

Can you make it through the thorn maze?

"Jesus...
Your sweet Face
is for me, Heaven
on earth."

"This is how He chooses to show His love".

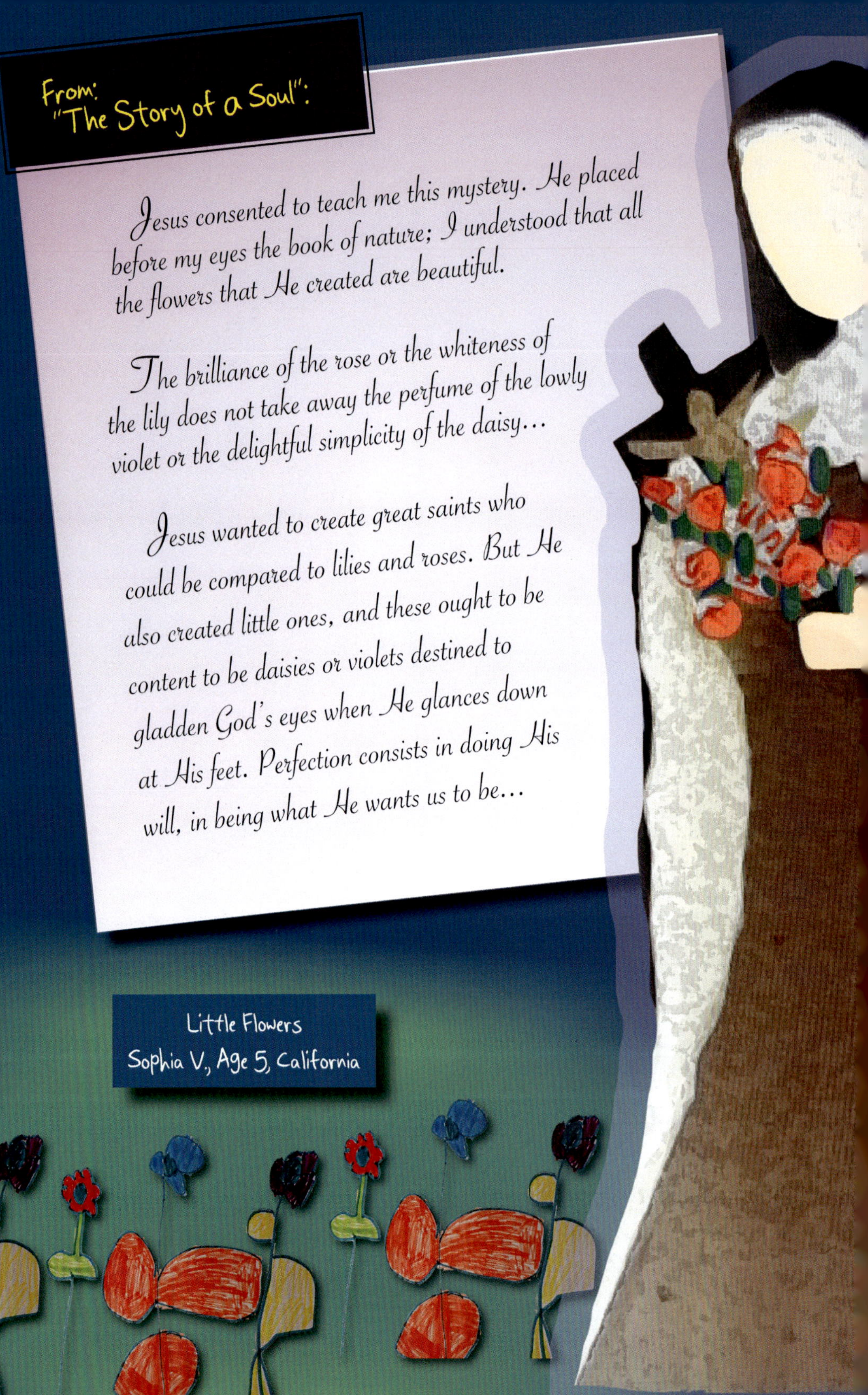
From:
"The Story of a Soul":

Jesus consented to teach me this mystery. He placed before my eyes the book of nature; I understood that all the flowers that He created are beautiful.

The brilliance of the rose or the whiteness of the lily does not take away the perfume of the lowly violet or the delightful simplicity of the daisy…

Jesus wanted to create great saints who could be compared to lilies and roses. But He also created little ones, and these ought to be content to be daisies or violets destined to gladden God's eyes when He glances down at His feet. Perfection consists in doing His will, in being what He wants us to be…

Little Flowers
Sophia V., Age 5, California

I understood Our Lord's love is revealed also in the simplest soul who does not resist His grace in anything. He created the child who doesn't know anything and only cries. He created poor primitive persons who only have natural law as a guide, and it is to their hearts He consents to come down; here are wildflowers whose simplicity delights Him…

By bringing Himself low in this way, God shows His infinite greatness Just as the sun shines at the same time on tall cedars and on each flower as if it were the only one on earth, in the same way Our Lord is concerned particularly for every soul as if there were none like it. And just as in nature all the seasons are arranged in such a way as to cause the humblest daisy to open on the appointed day, in the same way all things correspond to the good of each soul.

So, it is with happiness that I come to sing near you of the mercies of the Lord… I am going to write the story of the little flower picked by Jesus. It seems to me that if a little flower could talk, it would tell simply what God has done for it, without trying to hide its blessings.

Book of Saint
Bridget of Sweden's
Revelations,
1375 A.D.

O Sweet Jesus!

Pierce my heart so that my tears

of penitence and love will be my

bread day and night. May I be

converted entirely to Thee; may

my heart be Thy perpetual habitation;

may my conversation be pleasing

to Thee; and may the end of my life be

so praiseworthy that I may merit

heaven and there with Thy saints,

praise Thee forever. Amen.

- Saint Bridget of Sweden

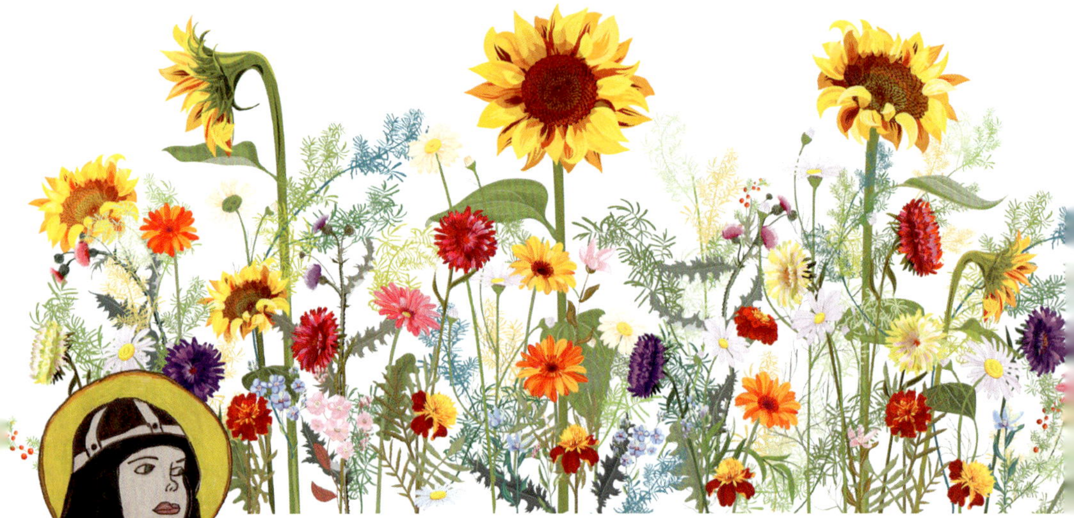

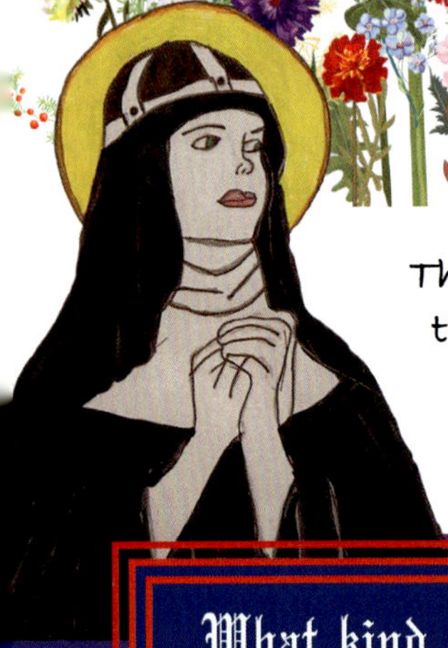

These flowers are all the chosen men from Adam to the end of the world which were planted in the garden of the world and shone and smelled in manifold virtues. - Saint Bridget of Sweden

What kind of flower do you think Saint Bridget is?

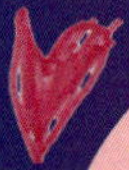

In seeking to imitate Mary, she made herself a faithful wife, mother and religious; in the Virgin's footsteps, she sought in every circumstance to do God's will without reserve.
- Pope John Paul II

Saint Bridget of Sweeden becamae a saint because She exercised a wide apostolate among rich and poor, sheltering the homeless and sinners, and She worked untiringly for the end of the Avignon papacy and for the Pope to return to Rome.

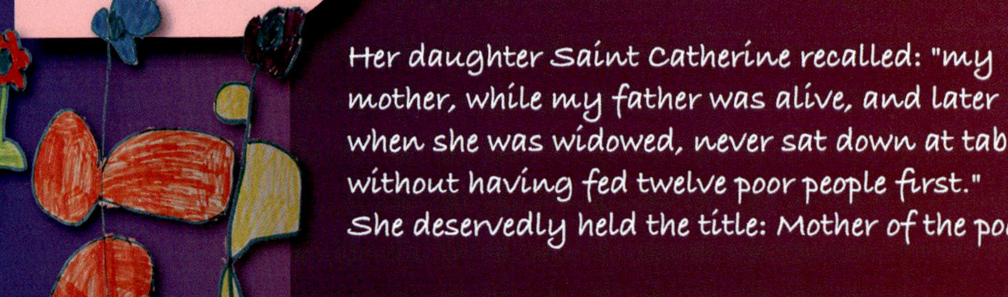

Her daughter Saint Catherine recalled: "my mother, while my father was alive, and later when she was widowed, never sat down at table without having fed twelve poor people first." She deservedly held the title: Mother of the poor.

Can you paint flowers in a vase?

Vincent Van Gogh, 1890 A.D.

Since the just man is planted in the house of our God, his leaves, flowers, and fruit grow there, and are dedicated to the service of the Divine Majesty. - Saint Francis De Sales

Do you know how flowers grow?

Can you grow a flower?

See how the farmer waits for the precious fruit of the earth, until it receives the early and the late rains. - Saint James

Picking Flowers,
Pierre-Auguste Renoir, 1875 A.D.

Patience

Above all trust in the slow work of God

Above All Trust in the Slow Work of God
Alyssa T, Age 9 & Maura A, Age 8, Wyoming

Love is
patient
& kind...

Do you know what
the twelve fruits of the
Holy Ghost are?

Answer: The twelve fruits of the Holy Ghost
are: Charity, Joy, Peace, Patience, Benignity,
Goodness, Long-suffering, Mildness, Faith,
Modesty, Continency, and Chastity.

French newspapers told the story of Henri Pranzini, convicted of the brutal murder of two women and a child. For months, Saint Thérèse prayed for his conversion, so that his soul could be saved, yet Pranzini showed no remorse. At the end of August, the newspapers reported that just as his neck was placed on the guillotine, he had grabbed a crucifix and kissed it three times. Saint Thérèse believed that her prayers had helped save him. She continued to pray for him after his death.

St. Thérèse during prayer sat in front of a Sister who fidgeted and made noise. She wanted to turn round, and make her stop; but in her heart Saint Thérèse knew that she should bear it patiently. She wrote: "After a time I tried to endure it in peace and joy, and I strove to take actual pleasure in the disagreeable little noise. Instead of trying not to hear it, which was impossible, I set myself to listen, as though it had been some delightful music, and my meditation was passed in offering this music to Our Lord."

How is a butterfly an example of patience?

How do you practice patience?

"When
very little, these
words gave me courage,
and even now, in spite
of the years which have
put to flight so many
impressions of childish piety,
the image of the ship still
charms my soul and helps it
put up with its exile."
- Saint Thérèse

"And as a ship that passes through the waves: when it is gone by, the trace cannot be found, nor the path of its keel in the waters."

-Wisdom

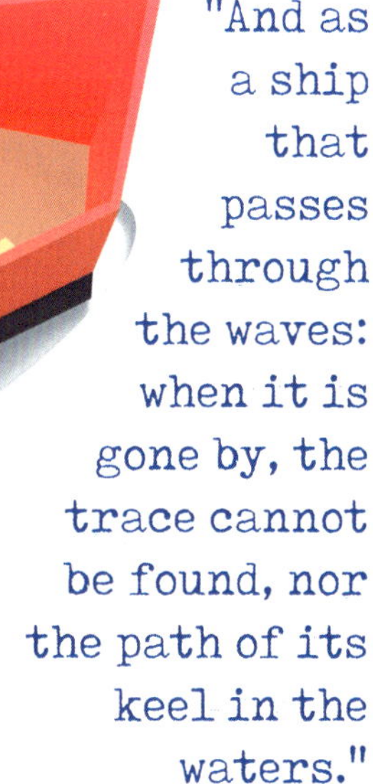

"When I think of these things, my soul is plunged into infinity, and it seems to me that it already touches the eternal shore. I seem to be receiving the embraces of Jesus."

Saint Thérèse died on September 30, 1897. On her deathbed, she is reported to have said: "I have reached the point of not being able to suffer any more, because all suffering is sweet to me."
Her last words were: "My God, I love you!"

Eternal life consists in the Beatific Vision. The vision of God face to face. This is the reward promised to the children of God.

In order for the blessed to see Him face to face, God enlightens them by "lumen gloriae", the light of glory. To the vision of God is added the possession of God through the bonds of the most perfect love. Unspeakable happiness is theirs.

"Eye hath not seen, nor ear heard, neither hath it entered into the heart of man, what things God hath prepared for them that love Him." - Saint Paul

They are united in the most intimate love to the glorified Humanity of Christ with His Blessed Mother, with all the Angels and Saints.

All the blessed see God face to face, some however, more pefectly than others, according to the degree of their merit.

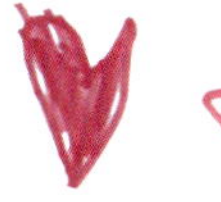

"Every man shall receive his own reward according to his own labor."
- Saint Paul

Yet, all are perfectly content and happy rejoicing in another's happiness and blessing the justice of God.

– Father John Laux

From "Story of a Soul":

I was surprised that God didn't give equal glory to all the Elect in heaven, and I was afraid all would not beperfectly happy. Then my sister told me to fetch Papa's large cup and set it alongside my thimble and she filled both to the brim with water. She asked me which one was fuller. I said that each was as full as the other and it was impossible to put in more water than they could contain. I understand that in heaven God will grant His Elect as much glory as they can take, the last having nothing to envy in the first.

The Saints want to help us get to heaven too! Saint Thérèse promised to send a "shower of roses" to all those who she helps!

I love the thorns that guard the rose

If you seek patience, you will find no
better example than the cross.
Great patience occurs in two ways:
either when one patiently suffers much,
or when one suffers things which one is
able to avoid and yet does not avoid.
Christ endured much on the cross, and did
so patiently, because when He
suffered He did not threaten;
He was led like a sheep to the slaughter
and He did not open His mouth.
-Saint Thomas Aquinas

Mary, Mystical Rose

Teach us to be like you!

Oh Mary, my Queen and my mother, I give myself entirely to thee. To show my devotion to thee, I consecrate to thee this day my eyes, my ears, my mouth, my heart, my whole being without reserve. Wherefore, good mother, as I am thine own, keep me and guard me as thy property and possession.

Eve, Mother of Mankind
Pray for us!

Saint Bridget of Sweden
Pray for us!

Saint Thérèse of Lisieux
Pray for us!

Did you
enjoy
this book?

Do you want to
see your artwork
or writing
featured
in an upcoming
book?
Go to: x-iota.com

Bonus Content after credits!

All original
and kid-submitted artwork
and text belongs to:
X-Iota Development

Oh, By Gabriel's "Ave,"
Uttered Long Ago,
Eva's Name Reversing,
Established Peace Below...

Thérèse von Lisieux – Unknown photographer,
Public domain, via Wikimedia Commons

Fotografía mortuoria de Santa Teresa de Lisieux – Unknown,
Public domain, via Wikimedia Commons

Verkündigung, Gabriel – Ausschnitt & Trestina,
CC BY-SA 4.0, via Wikimedia Commons

Verkündigung, Maria – Ausschnitt & Trestina,
CC BY-SA 4.0, via Wikimedia Commons

Virgen Del Rosario – Domingo Martínez,
Public domain, via Wikimedia Commons

Bibliography:

Ad Caeli Reginam. (October 11, 1954). Pope Pius XII. The Holy See.
Accessed online at: https://www.vatican.va/content/pius-xii/
en/encyclicals/documents/
hf_p-xii_enc_11101954_ad-caeli-reginam.html

Adam, Eve & the Paradise Tree. (n.d.). Elaine Jordan.
Tradition in Action. Accessed online at:
https://www.traditioninaction.org/religious/f031_Tree.htm

Baltimore Catechism. (1891). Cathechism. The Catholic Primer
(2005 – digital). Accessed online at: https://www.catechism.cc/
catechisms/Baltimore_Catechism.pdf

Chief Truths of the Faith. (1990). Fr. John Laux.
TAN Books. Rockford, IL

City of God. Mary of Agreda. Blatter.
Accessed online at: https://archive.org/download/
mysticalcityofgo01dejauoft/mysticalcityofgo01dejauoft.pdf

Cross Exemplifies Every Virtue. (Jan 26, 2021).
St. Thomas Aquinas. Original work: Colatio 6 super
Credo in Deum. Accessed online at:
https://www.crossroadsinitiative.com/media/articles/
thecrossexemplifieseveryvirtue/

Douay Rheims Bible. (2019 edition). Loreto Publications.
Originally Published 1609. Accessed online at: www.drbo.org

Litany of Loreto. (n.d.). The Holy See.
Accessed online at: https://www.vatican.va/special/
rosary/documents/litanie-lauretane_en.html

Mary as the Mystical Rose. (June 20, 2020). Fr. Cassian Sama, O.P.
The Dominican Province of St. Albert the Great.
Accessed online at: https://www.maryscrown.org/post/
mary-as-the-mystical-rose Mystical City of God. (1914). Venerable

Mystici Corporis Christi. (June 29, 1943). Pope Pius XII. The Holy See.
Accessed online at: https://www.vatican.va/content/pius-xii/en/
encyclicals/documents/hf_p-xii_enc_29061943_
mystici-corporis-christi.html

Mystical Flora. (1891). St. Francis de Sales. Mulholland (TR).
M. H. Gill and Son. Dublin. Accessed online at:
http://www.saintsbooks.net/books/St.%20Francis%20de%20Sales
%20-%20Mystical%20Flora%20or%2The%20Christian%20Life%20
under%20the%20Emblem%20of%20Plants.pdf

The Mystical Rose. (1996). John Henry Newman. Scepter Publishers.
Originally published: 1955. St. Paul Publications. NY.

The Prophecies and Revelations of Saint Bridget (Birgitta) of Sweden.
(n.d.). Saints Books. Accessed online at: http://www.saintsbooks.net/
books/St.%20Bridget%20(Birgitta)%20of%20Sweden%20-%
20Prophecies%20and%20Revelations.html

Saint Bridget. (n.d.). The Fifteen St. Bridget Prayers revealed by
Our Lord to Saint Bridget of Sweden in the Church of St. Paul at Rome.
Reprinted in Pieta Prayer Book. (2006).

Saint Bridget: A Unique Model Of Feminine Holiness. (October 9, 2002).
Pope John Paul II. L'Osservatore Romano. The Vatican.
Accessed online at:https://www.catholicculture.org/culture
/library/view.cfm?id=4507

Story of a Soul. (2010). St. Thérèse of Lisieux. TAN Books.

Mary loves Roses

She makes use of them

as a sign of

her presence.

Did you know?
The black
ribbon
around
Mary's waist
shows that
she is
expecting
a child.

Our Lady of Guadalupe

God the Father
fashioning the
image of the
Virgin. 1800 A.D.

The image had been
painted in one step
with no sketches or
corrections and no
visible brush strokes.

On the Feast of the Immaculate
Conception, Saint Juan Diego was
crossing Tepeyac Hill on
his way to Mass, when
he heard heavenly
music. A beautiful
voice from a
mysterious lady
was calling out to
Juan. Unafraid, he approached her.
She asked that a church be built
in her honor. Juan gathered roses,
which Mary told him to give to the
bishop as a sign. When Juan went to
show the bishop the roses, a
miraculous image of Our Lady
appeared on his tilma.

The flowers on
Mary's tunic are a
map of the local hills
and rivers at the time
of her appearance.

The stars on her
mantle are in the
exact position of the
constellations on
December 12, 1531.

Her mantle also
shows that she is
royalty since only
the native emperors
wore that color.

Mary appears on the tilma as the Woman
in the Angels' vision: about to give birth,
clothed with the sun, and the moon at her feet.

In 1936, a sample of the fabric
indicated that the pigments
used were from no known
source, whether animal, mineral,
or vegetable.